Discipline

JANE YEH was born in America and has lived in London since 2002. She holds degrees in English and Creative Writing from Harvard, Iowa, Manchester Metropolitan, and Royal Holloway London universities. Her first collection of poems, *Marabou* (Carcanet, 2005), was shortlisted for the Whitbread, Forward, and Aldeburgh poetry prizes. She was named a Next Generation poet by the Poetry Book Society for her second collection, *The Ninjas* (Carcanet, 2012). A Lecturer in Creative Writing at the Open University, she also writes on books, theatre, and fashion for such publications as *The Poetry Review* and *The Village Voice*.

First published in Great Britain in 2019 by
Carcanet
Alliance House, 30 Cross Street
Manchester, M2 7AQ
www.carcanet.co.uk

A CIP catalogue record for this book is
available from the British Library.
ISBN 978 1 78410 707 9

Book design by Andrew Latimer
Printed in Great Britain by SRP Ltd, Exeter, Devon

The publisher acknowledges financial
assistance from Arts Council England.

Discipline

JANE YEH

CARCANET

Acknowledgements

Sincere thanks to the editors of the anthologies, publications, and websites where some of these poems first appeared: *Alphabeast* (Type Hike, 2019); *Birdbook: Saltwater and Shore* (Sidekick Books, 2016); *Boston Review*; *Cold Fire: Poetry Inspired by David Bowie* (The Rialto, 2017); *For Every Year*; *Granta*; *Metamorphic: 21st Century Poets Respond to Ovid* (Recent Work Press, 2017); *The New Republic*; *The New York Review of Books*; *PN Review*; *Poems in Which*; *Poetry* (Chicago); *Poetry London*; *The Poetry Review*; *Spells: 21st Century Occult Poetry* (Ignota Books, 2018); *tremble: The University of Canberra Vice-Chancellor's International Poetry Prize 2016* (International Poetry Studies Institute, 2016); *'Why Poetry?': The Lunar Poetry Podcasts Anthology* (Verve Poetry Press, 2018); and *Wretched Strangers* (Boiler House Press, 2018).

Grateful thanks also to those who commissioned the following: 'Utopia Villas' was commissioned by the Bristol Festival of Ideas for the Contemporary Poets and Utopia project, Bristol. 'Installation' was commissioned by the Spanish Contemporary Art Network to accompany the exhibition 'Miseratione Non Mercede' at Copperfield Gallery, London. 'Rabbit Empire' was commissioned by Rachel Long for the Lit and Lynch: *Inland Empire* project at Hackney Picturehouse, London.

Lastly, many thanks to my friends and family for their support.

Contents

III

Discipline

I

A Short History of Style

Joey Arias at Jackie 60, New York, 1997

The disposition of her arms
Is a case of

Nothing ventured, nothing
Gained. Her violet ear

Makes sense if
Something wicked is

Being said. The angle
Of her nose is a challenge,

A crime against nature. Her
Throat a fine line. *Lover*

Where have you been?
Mistakes come back to her

Like wrong notes, a clarinet
Of echoes. You can take the boy

Out of Dubuque… Nothing
Like bourbon

To make her sing
A slow tune: downcast

Eyes, hands swaying
Just so. The catch

In her voice like a rusty key
Turned. A hundred

Nights blurred together
Like an ink blot

Smeared – her long fall
Of hair saying *No no no.*

A Short History of Migration

We boarded a seashell to ride across the waves.
The mythology of our passage involved dirt, sharks, a zeppelin, and wires.
We ate the same meal seventeen days in a row (pancakes).
We learned to say yes, please in four different languages.

Our fur-lined hats were useless in the fine September air.
The mystery of our parentage was a serape on our backs.
On the prairie, the locals tried to take us at face value.
We learned about sturgeon, washing machines, ennui, and fake tan.

We joined a fruit-of-the-month club to widen our horizons.
The mastery of our foliage required an endless sea of mowing.
We attended bake sales with a suspicious degree of fervour.
We hindered our children with violins, bad haircuts, and diplomas.

Our names were changed to make them easier to remember.
The monastery of our heritage was repurposed into handy snacks.
We sold refrigerators to people who already had refrigerators.
We lived in suburban glory in our off-plan townhouses.

Our children were changed to make them meaner and fatter.
The memory of our verbiage was as a schnitzel in the wind.
We kept our money close, and our feelings closer.
In the event of an emergency, we kept a baseball bat prepared.

Discipline

The shape of a deer
In silhouette

Projected on a woman's dress. Off
With her arms, her head – the mark

Of a hoof in snow, superimposed
On a high heel, a pool of milk;

The lines converge
And part like migrating birds. Her skirt

Is an hourglass
Filling up with stones. Her heart

Is a caveat. *See how they run.*
If her foot

Points towards the past,
It's called composition. (Too much

Thinking spoils a fawn.) Her
Secrets play on continuous loop,

Like a B-movie. On
The reverse: a blank surface

Painted over – another girl,
Blotted out.

A Short History of Silence

In our house, all the clocks are turned off and the mirrors
Don't work. We sit like bread in a stay-fresh wrapper,
Keep ourselves to our *selves*. Sometimes the speeches
Are so beautiful it hurts. On the porch where we can't be

Seen to smile, the honeysuckle meshes with silent
Weeds. We rock back and forth, back and forth in our long
Black dresses. Mosquitoes taste our blood and find it good.

Inside, candles are lit every night and keep going
Until they burn themselves down. We kiss our fingers
To our lips like Italians, promise we'll never look back.
Whip-poor-will. When the doorbell rings we don't answer.

In winter, the fur grows long on the horses and the ice
Grows long on the eaves. We sleep in the same bed
Like good animals, braid our hair together, tailor
Our limbs to fit. *Conspiracy of wood.*

A Short History of Violence

The rush of air.
The fear

Is black and white,
A blur

Just over his head, a feathered
Ball of bad dreams

And someone shouting. A body
Just wants to mind himself,

Keep a blind eye. Out back
A string of lights

Pierces the horizon;
The ground races away

Beneath. He's
Been running for miles

In his ripped jeans, strips
Of T-shirt flapping, dirt

Like a rumour all over him.
His arm a bent lesson

In obedience – not enough.
Out here

Boys are ten a penny,
One less ain't worth

Spilt milk. The pulse
In his throat

Is a bridle against his skin.
The tyre tracks, the smell

Of burning – he can't outrun
The smoke at his back,

Like a panic
Rising. His body

A lamb sheared.

A Short History of Destruction

In the palace of the cats, we minused and gnawed.
We burrowed and simulated, skirting the wormholes.
In the shiny halls, cubist paintings looked down on us
Like startled Martians; lavish flower arrangements loomed
From the persistent étagères. Our peril

Was molten and diabolical, with a side of *told you so*.
Our children vanished and reappeared under different names.
All day, cats covered in gold sat in their perpendicular chairs
Planning invasions. In the padded drawing-rooms
They ate statement salads and filed their nails.

Item: Beshrew areas of carpet or supernumerary globes.
Item: The case of M., who was flattened by a ewer.
Each day, the smell of cat wafted malevolently through the cracks
In the platinum ceiling. We cowered and filleted
In our synthetic beds. The glamour of the cats

Was undeniable, like their long and curling hair.
They rinsed their paws in lemon-scented finger bowls
Between fish courses. A potpourri of tiny bells
Rang out silkily whenever one of them passed by.
We did covet and die many times

In the palace of the cats. Beneath the jagged
Candelabras, with our backward fur and shifty eyes,
We were killed like children. The antlers on the wall
Were implacable as Valkyries. Some of the cats
Played drastic minuets on diminutive grand pianos.

A Short History of Mythology

To be a lady centaur

                    leaping across the Hedgehog Isles

Is to be in heaven

                    and wearing a tropical lei

Like a shower of spiral curls

                    my tail is springy

It smells like violets and shit

                    in a good way

Thank you pool

                    I can bounce down a peninsula

Laden with Gorgonzola

                    harvesting bites between watching my shows

And inventing the handsaw

                    between weaving a tapestry

And visiting space

                    I will stomp on a few thousand years

Of lady centaur history

                    without regrets

To leap through a waterfall

                    in a novelty T-shirt

Holding a gift basket between my teeth

                    to shake my legs around

Pretending to be a freaky spider

                    to investigate a mole all day

Or whatever is stealing my tomatoes

                    is a paradise

Like a partridge

                    my head bobs when I run

My boobs bob when I run

                    when I run into the purple-tinged hills

I can be mythical

                                 like the very specific flower

They use in salads in L.A.

                                        as a garnish

If you look at it upside down

                                        you can see the face of a furious boy

A Short History of Patience

The soft chiffon of the river as it turns
Out of view. The woodpecker's stutter saying
Wish you were here. The birch branches tangled
Like wires overhead, sending mixed messages

To the birds. Baby, I could go out on a limb
And say the evening's smoky eye draws near,
The floorboards creak like a harpsichord played wrong,
The kettle rumbles with anticipation, then

Shuts itself off. Honey, without you it's cold
As a warthog's bare bottom, or the draught
That slips in under the door. Without you
I'm lonesome as a cricket in a jam jar, chirping

Till all the air runs out. *Won't you come home?*
Says the dustpan to the wandering broom.
Catch as catch can say the weeds to the scythe.
Ryegrass spreading through the yard like an open secret.
The blue line of the horizon like an eyelid, closed.

Self-Portrait as Joey Arias, Klaus Nomi, and Others

The curl of a dahlia is preposterous as the pancetta of my hair.
A streetlight posing as an innocent bystander; everything looks different
Behind closed doors. The hellacious cheeseburger of morn.

I twist my hand back and forth, but everything stays the same.
Which part of the dance is the hard part? All of it!
At the club: nobody talks to me, they are all afraid.

Even a fern has feelings. The nature of attraction is half fluke,
Half fiction. Medallion, leotard, leotard, beard. We don't want
Any trouble, but my face looks like this for a reason.

The past is another planet. Our sequinned dreams. The high falsetto
Of my squirrel friends. Or the time I grew a fringe –
Holy *merde*. My imaginary boyfriend was named Adolfo Jones.

How long is a piece of rope? I live in a small, dirty hospital
Full of talking machines. I live in an escape room no one has solved.
Beneath the city is another city, where everything matches us.

The Detectives

No matter where we go, it always looks like California.
Get in the car and drive. Our invisible friend
Comes with us everywhere, like a shadow.
He tells us how to keep moving on. We're haunted

By news of the absurd, by doors without locks, by bottles
Rattling in six-packs like bones. The game of
What's behind the dumpster. The game of *Don't be*
Such a dick. Behind every door is another

Motel room: light as a feather, stiff as a board,
No place for the weary. By the time you read this
We'll be gone. We can play air guitar for hours.
We can go anywhere, as long as it's east.

The needle points a finger, the birds in the sky
Make a V, the road to hell is paved with fresh
Burritos. The case of *The unwashed thermos.* The case
Of *Sit and spin.* Behind every day is another

Freaking day: run and gun, trail of breadcrumbs,
The bureau of shrunken heads. We study the book
Where all the words are written down. We follow
The script. There are more endings than we remember.

Utopia Villas

In our utopia, the oysters always sing.
There is a metronome the colour of Sacré-Coeur.
There is a messenger opening a secret scroll (good news).
In our lazy maisonette, we count the days until summer.

Pizza will come in two sizes: snack and preposteroso.
Poetic cockapoos will serenade us with their thoughts
While beseeching looks shoot out of their eyes like lasers.
In the strongholds of the North, a Cumberland sausage will rise

While a slain avocado comes back to life as guacamole (good karma).
We will spread out everywhere and chill like a floppy omelette.
We will be meticulous in love, ornithology, and dance.
Long avenues of deer will part like magic

In the sentimental sunlight. When we kiss,
Magpies will burst into song like a chorus of witches.

Self-Portrait as Klaus Nomi in New York

My mechanics are almost entirely self-taught. My super-scream capabilities,
My mythological silence. On television I look very smart.

Night falls like a slab of bacon. Every night is a performance
The diameter of a wire. In the mouth of a dog, the mouth of a god?

Every performance is a boulder to look behind. On the plastic grass
We hold a secretive ball. The ice cubes are enormous and come in different
      colours.

If I had my own planet it would be painted white; I'm modernist
Like that. My signature scent is L'air du prawn.

In my Freudian polo-neck, I watched a programme about regret.
This line is for a thought about film cinematography.

Every day is like a horse I don't want to ride – corduroy,
Corduroy, corduroy. If you pull the right string, the curtain will fall.

In an imaginary cab, you might pull the right string. Every line
Is a performance that won't stay up. My kingdom for a joke.

II

Events of 1871

My beloved oleomargarine, the struggle is real. Long-haired cats are assembling in the Crystal Palace. It feels like the century is just beginning. It feels like being slapped in the face with corrugated cardboard.

If you could see a million birds massed over San Francisco for a day, you might start to believe in magnetic fields. It feels like a massacre, but you don't know about the century. If you were being shot out of a cannon for the amusement of spectators, you might start to believe in hard luck. It feels like being slapped in the face with a cat. There are detectives in New Jersey investigating the circumstances.

If you could put an Apache chief on trial, you might be a wasichu. How soft, how melting is my oleaginous cube. There are fish who need protection by the American government. They're queuing out to Forest Hill. If you believe in progress, corrugated cardboard might be invented.

A mob of 500 men is no substitute for butter. If you feel like a human cannonball, you might believe in chop suey. I could be hanged for being in L.A. with my salmon. If you feel like setting fire to Chicago, you might put be on trial. There are Black Masons forming a lodge in New Jersey, which is progress.

A Short History of Childhood

Leaves brush against the window like fingers in the heat.
It's 1982. Summer holidays. Prison is a house
With all the windows shut, medley of sweat
And boredom. Carpets itchy under my bare feet.

I learn algebra from a foreign textbook, make bread
No one eats. The telly is an encyclopaedia
Of frosted makeup and panting kisses. x + y =
Thank you, ma'am. Information swells in my chest like yeast.

Insects buzz in the night, loud as a choir.
Lawns multiply down the empty street. My hair
Is a comedy of frizz and errors, big
As a soufflé. It takes me years to outgrow it.

Turn It On

Spill of sequins
Down the front.

Follow spot – coloured
French peacock. The song

Spills from her open
Mouth, don't you

Worry honey, left
Hand on the strings.

Her voice
Is a holler

Made of fury and beer.
Her lungs are a calamity –

Can't stand the thought. Chitchat
And sassafras. Light,

Then dark. Flip a switch.
Noise like a tidal wave

Swallowing her up, noise
Like a wall, hard

Heart pulling out all
The stops till it

Doesn't hurt
Any more. Don't *say*

The word. A chain
Of notes in the dark.

Won't she or will. The kick
And stutter of her voice

As the next song
Starts, her arm all

Guitar – sparkle and dirt.

Poem In Which All the Questions Are Answered

Next time, the last time really will be the last time.
The astrology column is written by a computer program in Stoke.
'Out of the mouths of babes' doesn't mean what people think it means.
Where there's a will, there's a dead body and a guilty-looking capybara.

For these questions: ellipsis, Jeffersonian, South American toad.
If you wait long enough, everything will come back at the same time.
Where there's smoke, there's an ex-smoker bumming other people's
        cigarettes.
Nothing is made in Middlesbrough but baked beans and disappointment.

'Tit for tat' doesn't mean what some people think it means.
Where there's hope, there's a poet with an unpublished memoir.
Acid-wash denim is bleached in the tears of spinsters.
Never underestimate the speed of a hungry walrus.

You can't hurry love (except on Saturday night in Doncaster).
Organised religion was invented as a stand-in for roast beef.
Spectacled bear, mirepoix, 57% of adult men.
When it's over, you can pretend you never cared about it anyway.

Happy Hour, New York City

The maxidress of the afternoon sags like cheap jersey
As the first margarita is shaken and poured. The heat
Is a blanket smothering all thought, is an abominable
Sauna room the size of a city; the steady drip
Of air-conditioning units pools on the sidewalk.
We clink our plastic glasses together, duel with tiny umbrellas.

The cinnamon bun of the conversation
Unspools till all the gossip is gone – Maxine of the office,
Our Lady of Scandals, Fernando of the enormous
Nose. Another round. The strawberry daiquiris
Melt like pink slush in the sunlight's glare.
In the unfathomable depths of the popcorn bowl

Lie the answers to all life's questions: what are
We here for? (Cheap drinks.) Day drains from the sky
Like the contents of a highball glass. A succession
Of dogs comes out to be walked before dinner.
The traffic stops and goes past, a mechanical river.
A siren goes off in the distance somewhere, like somebody crying.

Thanksgiving, New York City

The wild turkeys should be worried this year –
Their luscious free-range thighs are coveted
By every chef in the city. The cornucopia
Of tubers at the Greenmarket stand
Is a tumultuous mob of spectators, jostling
For position. Decorative gourds invade shops
Like misshapen aliens; a mountain of cookbooks
Sprouts on the kitchen counter. You could stab
A ham with all the advice you've been given.

Where the pie plates buckle, there buckle I.
The metaphysical weight of the potluck dinner
Makes muffins of us all. On the sideboard lurk
The candied yams of no one's dreams, uneaten
Bowls of stuffing. The TV chatters to itself
Like a crazy uncle, the moon fills the sky
Like a ripening cheese. We could sit here
Till the cows come home, if we didn't have
Work tomorrow. The marshmallow fluff
Of your cerebellum says *go to sleep.*

These Movies

The story of this movie can't be described in words. This movie is like when you suddenly pull off a wig to reveal another wig underneath, which you were wearing all along. (The second wig has a flatter hairstyle but is clearly still a wig.) This movie is like how horses have only four possible gaits, except for horses in Iceland, which have a fifth gait, but it doesn't matter because they aren't ever allowed to leave the country. This movie is like the story of the Thracian liar, a Thracian man who was incapable of lying. (This is a paradox.) This story is like the movie of a sewing machine sewing a teacup while a teacup printed with sewing machines looks on. This movie is like the feeling of a glass slowly overflowing because you keep pouring water into it no matter what. (And also like the overflowing water.) I don't really rate this movie.

This movie is another movie that can't be described in words, even though a number of treatments were written to describe it. This movie was shown in the context of numerous other movies that featured exploding flowers, a spinning bicycle wheel, and ostriches as heroes. In such a movie-ish context, this movie appeared to be like a bird eating poisonous roses leaf by leaf, or else like a carton of automatic pencils gathering dust, or like an elegant lady in a mantilla plucking her eyebrows badly. If this movie could talk, it would have a squeaky voice like a nerd in a Hollywood movie, even though most nerds actually have normal voices. Whatever happens in this movie is valid, like the way Newtonian physics can predict the movement of smoke from the tip of a lit cigarette. The end of this movie could've been made by a dog pressing its nose into wet concrete over and over. Good movie.

Pacific Pocket Mouse

It isn't easy being so small   that your head is the size of a marble
Rolling across the floor please   don't step on me my tiny paws
Are digging a tunnel the size of your thumb   (it's called a burrow
My home)   even though I'm small I have rights
Like the right to keep any nuts   I find like the way I like
To go out at night and stuff my face   with seeds (literally
I store them in my cheeks to eat later   my private larder)
Even though we're so small   they call us a mischief
A harvest or horde we're just   trying to stay alive
In your sandy scrub (please   ignore us sneaky ants and foxes)
Even though my voice is very small   like the sound of a miniature beeper
Going off   I am talking to you now mouse to mouse
Like an imaginary phone   in El Segundo please
Remember my silky fur how I don't   have a fire helmet to protect
My tiny skull how I'm still   here even though you think you're alone

Scenes From Sherlock Holmes and the Pearl of Death

1. Following on from a horse collar
2. Ensconced at home with tuxedo cat
3. Rollmops
4. The glass dome of night, momentarily lifted
5. Ready or not, a mesomorph comes
6. Behind the splendour of Crabby Mountain
7. Unpleasant emission from a malapert plover
8. Far from the light of sweet seabirds
9. Where the crumbs go

10. Big cheese + old bag + interval = gabfest
11. Spreading the net, waggling the fingers
12. Dead end is to dogleg as cursory is to smokeless
13. A missive from the mysterious East (i.e., East Grinstead)
14. Enter a mandarin
15. Hog-tied, railroaded, softsoaped, and rifled
16. In the belly of the well of the pergola of doom
17. To cover with gold stars, or glitterpalooza
18. How we became angels

19. Up periscope vs. open sesame
20. The indivisible wall between the living and the dead
21. As gullible as a bowl full of honey
22. Exit on milk float, pursued by sausage dog
23. *Oy vey can you see?*
24. For the last time, humming a Milanese song
25. For the last time, per the ferocious chasm of yearning
26. Dumpling Village, Oxfordshire (twinned with Flushing)
27. No more llamas?

A Monstrous Regiment of Women

My uniform was gabardine brown, with extra straps attached.
I wheedled the shit out of the target. I Mumbai'd his sorry ass
All over the pavement. *Don't believe the lies they tell.*

My ornamental shrubs were planted for maximum effect.
I took a bullet right in the pitta pocket. I kebabed
And weaved back to camp. *Don't look down.*

The lessons were relentless, but no one lost a head.
I could chipolata like a mother without skipping a beat.
I could shake a tail, cobra-style. We saddled up

The Thighmaster and rolled into town – *Hey baby, nice veal.*
This is what we train for: the wicked *thwack* and fall.
I pocketed the nunchucks and cleared the scene.

I manacled a sandwich and totted up the score.
Sisters, I think our kindness will surprise them
When the time for judgement comes.

Rejected Book Reviews

In this book the main character is a serial killer or a nun. The *mise en place* is reminiscent of a small bowl of baby carrots next to a vinegar cruet. The cruet is the storyline about a reckless underwear magnate reduced to foraging for change, while the carrots are the subplot in which a professional mime artist falls in love with her separated-at-birth evil twin. You won't believe how many readers liked this book. The pace of the book is like a nun being followed by a disdainful alpaca, or an oversized yacht being towed by a grateful SUV. Apart from the ending, the book's structure seems to be based on the mediaeval prose travel legend *Rompers A-Rove*, with its episodic plodding and semi-metallic verse. This book cannot be recommended more highly.

By contrast, this other book will not appeal to your emotions one bit. If it were a character in a movie, it would be a non-speaking waiter in the back of a Scandinavian restaurant kitchen in Slough. The main characteristics of this book are a distinctly tomato-ey ambience, numerous false fronts, and the desire to relocate to a particoloured island. Other things this book made me think of are the population of Zanzibar and the number of stripes in a metre of tie-stripe silk – good stuff. If you were to run over this book with a lightweight convertible, it would resemble a blueberry pancake where the blueberries are the book's themes leaking their juices all over the pavement. The disappointment you'll feel after finishing this book is probably equal to the intense unease of an experienced postal carrier faced with an address that doesn't exist. Clearly this book is essential beach reading.

Self-Portrait With Cat

This morning I was bitten and scratched in my bed, an unwelcome practice. There is a dignity in being the victim of a creature without speech. The sound of a distant audience came across the wire, a room full of invisible people in another city. When I was little, I had more imagination and made dresses for my toy dog named Pepsi.

Only certain breeds of cats can be trained. There is a device timed to go off in eight minutes. If you could see an absent friend again, what would you give? My pantry contains freeze-dried coffee and four types of rice. I used to live on instant noodles before I developed a more sophisticated palate.

Every day is like pulling on a pair of Spanx, sometimes easier, sometimes not. The weather in my satin boudoir is always the same. I look at a cat's balls, a polychrome table, and a pond in Essex on a screen. I require a high salt content to function correctly. If the right moment has passed, would I know it?

There is a four-way conversation about shingles and adding potatoes to dough. Despite my desire for knowledge, I don't listen. My brain is like a *marron glacé*, sugared and crumbling. If my attention span were any shorter —. Through the window, more windows.

III

Self-Portrait as a Spinster

The macadamia nut of sunset blanketed with a strawberry breeze.
Such moments are infrequent in our sugar-substitute days.

Like the texture of a shiny wallpaper, without good taste.
So melodious in the pima cotton night is the song of the maidenhair cat.

To be unloved is like listening to a progress report on courgettes – for months.
My feelings, propelled in a Victorian swimming cage over a rocky beach.

I decanted my sincerity into a carefully-labelled trunk.
I wilted like a leftover chicken wing in the crispy light of day.

It was awful to be unloved, like having an embarrassing disease.
(Somewhere on the moon, a Clanger emits a distant, mournful chirp.)

I pretended to be carefree yet salty, like a seaside wench.
The Bakelite earring of summer swayed to and fro, to and fro.

It was okay to be alone, like a sausage in a garden full of flowers.
In the caramel air, a Labrador stared kindly at my meaty display.

Why I Am Not a Sculpture

To be a statue   carved by Bernini

Lounging in a climate-controlled museum in Rome   is luxury

Like the luxury of a personal pan pizza   with unlimited free toppings

Or the luxurious feel of a premium eye pencil   used to draw bisons on the walls of a French cave

To be so white and glossy   is unimaginable

Like how I imagine a plate of eggs painted by Velásquez   or the lid of a designer toilet cistern

In a European magazine   (I could be European

And wear a dashingly arranged scarf   or sip oddly-named liqueurs that taste like semen

In a Neoclassical palais)   but in the scheme of things

Where I am marble and still   my wrist will be a marvel

Like the marvel of an isthmus   whose name can only be pronounced if you have a lisp

Or the marvellous sausage   that saved a man from the Inquisition in 1582

It is definitely marvellous   to be as attenuated

As the casually extended leg of a greyhound
          reclining on its very own velvet settee
To be so thoroughbred
      is an accomplishment
Like the thoroughly flattened face of a Persian cat
          which always looks peevish
Or the extremely frivolous ceiling
     of a banqueting hall where royals are put to death
If it is admirable to be so luxurious
      then I will never be admired
The way a designer toilet cistern is admired
       or a piece of elaborate pâtisserie
(Although I am not a statue
     I have often held my arms aloft
As when catching a carelessly thrown baby
     or pointing at two meteors at the same time)
It is exhausting trying to be so inanimate
     and desirable
If my arm breaks off like the shell
     of a freshly-filled cannoli
You will know why

A Short History of Romance

1. As soon as the lights come on making of us a scene
2. The velvet of an imaginary tongue
3. Lake-effect cloud, ghost phone, down the glistening street
4. Night veils us (but the holes in my tights still show)

5. Under the arches, like an heirloom coverlet
6. As if the lights could be armour (or a cocktail dress)
7. Our reflections in windows like passing fancies
8. Matte brick lip, empty bottle, prone to shrieking

9. Part cream puff, part poison, part tranquiliser dart
10. In terms of lurking: half-moonlight at our throats
11. If I told you, I would have to kiss you
12. A shiver of bracelets guarding my arms

13. Huddled under heat lamps and their unrelenting gaze
14. Mini martini, cloaking device, autonomic response
15. Like falling off a ledge in the dark (only slower)
16. The sound of our breath in the unfurling night

Public House

Glitter in the trees.
Glitter and shadow. Leaves

Massing like birds or
Faces, clusters of people passing

Through the narrow
Streets, full of litter

And heroes. A serenade
Of buses down the road

From the spaceship
Library! Our incense

Is the smell of raw chicken
And tilapia in summer,

Our rough cassavas
Precious gems – no

Stopping between the hours of
Primark and Rizla, only dancing

On a reservoir on top of
The world: *look what*

The cat dragged in. Oh angels
Of Peckham, from the nail bars

To the Common, we sweep
Your fiery steps clean. The

Clink of glasses
Is found music, a belated

Poem: our temple to lager
And order, archive

Of dogs lost, old
House holding our stories between

Its boards (*please*
Respect the neighbours). In

This ragged and ordinary
Palace, our voices merge

Like rustling leaves. The way
A dozen tea lights make

A constellation: stars
In the dark, our collective dreams.

True Facts About the Herring Gull

The cries of the herring gull sound like a small barking dog.
I like to see a gull perched on a railing or a chair.
Gulls will eat bread, rotten fruit, crisps, and even vomit.
One of their cries means *This is my piece of food.*

If a herring gull approaches you, be somewhat afraid.
A gull in every pot and a herring in every chamber.
The ulterior motives of gulls are like Wotsits trapped in crystal.
They can stand atop spikes due to their super-leathery soles.

If gulls were horses, burgers would ride.
Their natures are capricious like that of a small beautiful dog.
Gull me not, lest ye be shat on by a gull.
Of the language of the gulls, we must remain silent. (*pause*)

Most of their cries mean *Give me your chips.*
In the company of gulls, a cockle is as good as a smile.
The long-term plans of gulls are like the space in a box full of concrete.
If in doubt, placate a gull by singing of its mother.

The Rhinos

We meet under the stars, touch noses
In the dark. Our secret greeting.

Our nocturnal meetings are brief, but friendly.
Sometimes I pretend to be asleep.

We really aren't
The loners you think. We snort and cluck
When we're together. Our private conversation.

The enchilada of Africa — the whole
Kalahari — is our kitchen.
I'm only interesting to smaller males.

We're not in a hurry
To copulate. I swing my head from side to side,
Then run away. It's called flirting.

Our dusty hides are thick, but sensitive.
I capture bugs by accident in my teeth.

By day we don't gather,
Just do our own thing. I poke my nose
In a mud hole, splash around in my piss.

I'd rather not have a bath
If I can help it. My powerful smell.

We're vanishing one by one
From the bare savannah.

Above, the high sky –
Our canopy, our heaven.

Installation

Bird hanging
From a taxidermy door.

One leg
Dangling. To install

A shoe,
Find a shoe

Missing a foot. The brass rail
Is for help. In the work

A wheel is taken apart,
The third bird

Hops the perimeter
Of floor, something spilt

Is a circle cut out
Of wood. If a boy could make

His own world
Like this, it would be safe

To go out. The Braille
Of his fingers reading

Another hand's shape.
Another foot

Without a leg –
Beautiful fragment. Nobody's

Coming to take you
To the ball. If a boy

Could be a bird –
Behind the door

Of his eyes, a crowd of words
Pressed mute. His hand

Is a book with the pages glued
Together; the sea

Is a circle that spits
Him out.

Eight Scenes From an Exhibition

1.

Big as a house,
Eyed up and down. A woman
Carved out of
A sugar block, gargantuan.
Around her heels bacteria form –
Slow and green, not a metaphor.

2.

In the weird rainbowland video
The artist is dressed as a cat.
She interviews herself, dressed
As someone else. In the underground lair
There are even more of her.
Scary dancing.

3.

Llamas in fog. Then the silent
Ride of Lycra, a mob
Of men on bicycles.
The llamas sit on the road,
Unbothered. In their heads
It's winter, no big deal.

4.

A line of text
Printed over and over again.
The posters curl on the floor,
Illegible – you can take one.
The words say something
About being American.
Block caps.

5.

Crochet Molotov cocktail.
Crochet bacon and eggs.
Display of sweets that would be in a corner
Shop, crocheted. The stitches
Perfectly even in allure, an armour
Of yarn, little miracle.

6.

The girls
Are looking down
At the bottom of the frame. Two heads
Identical – short curls, silvery cheeks pressed
Together. They might be crying.
Cut to letters on a cliff spelling ECHO.

7.

If you walk into the hole
Lined with feathers, it's a tunnel.
Birdsong and electronic
Voices, paper clocks.
When you leave, it's like being born –
A buzzer sounds, then nothing.

8.

On the blue and orange walls
She draws. Chalk
Is a rite, melancholy
Are flowers, under a sinister
River an invisible landscape
Grows. A road and a door.

Self-Portrait as New York in the Eighties

Brrring! I answer like a retro panther in my polyester sheath.
As long as I've got my hair I'll make it. Sweetness

In the air or on the streets, my city, *give us any chance...*
In the Pyramid only the good girls were real. Back-to-back

Like dancing might make us strong. We were poor
As a fake fur lined with fake fur, *no loco*, city of angles

And steel beams to bring our love to. Bring back the girls
We were before the story ended. I sweep like a flamingo

Into the velvety streets. *Catsuit city.* Sometimes my face
Is shorthand for a face. We were real before it was good

To be real, turned out like a girl seen *at an angle*,
Askance. Sweet, then sour. My lips the colour of Doubt.

Bel Canto

The opera
In her head

Runs with no interval,
A lot of people singing tunelessly

About the same things.
An overheard

Comment like
A rotting peach.

The overzealous
Cockatoo of her impatience,

Flap flap. The slab
Of blue behind her

Is a sea of
Her doubts. The squirrel

In her stomach
Trying to get out –

They say you have to be
Twice as good. They say

There are pills
For everything now. Enamel

Eyes to see all
The better with, my

Dear. Fur coat
For your tongue —

Rabbit Empire

In the empire of the rabbits, the long-eyed girl is king.
The afterlife is like a movie, edited
And full of plot holes. On a leatherette settee
We twitch our ears coquettishly. We think she loves us.

Green walls will with a green dress chime. The angora
Of our hearts softly blows, whenever she draws near.
The door to the past only opens one way,
Into a hotel room – you can't turn it off like TV.

It's swish to nibble on a cream cracker
While she goes about in heels like a bachelorette on speed.
At the picnic, the grass is so green we could cry.
The language of the dead sounds like static

Or a weird encyclopaedia; when the phone rings,
It's for her. Our eyes light up in the dark.
She wakes up in Kansas, trailing memories like babies.
Roses fall through the air like a sweet shop exploding.

Notes

'A Short History of Style': Joey Arias is a cabaret and drag artist best known for performing the songs of Billie Holiday. The opening of this poem was prompted by the painting *Portrait of Madame X* (1884), by John Singer Sargent.

'Discipline': The title is taken from the painting that initially prompted the poem, *Discipline* (2013), by Kirsten Glass.

'A Short History of Violence': The opening of this poem was prompted by the 2012 painting *Brujas en el Aire*, by José Carlos Naranjo.

'A Short History of Mythology': A few of the details here (the Hedgehog Isles, the invention of the handsaw, etc.) can be found in *Metamorphoses: A New Verse Translation*, by Ovid, translated by David Raeburn (Penguin, 2004).

'Self-Portrait as Joey Arias, Klaus Nomi, and Others': Klaus Nomi was a German performance artist and singer who was part of the New York club scene from the 1970s until his death in 1983.

'Events of 1871': This poem references actual events that occurred in 1871 in Britain and America, mostly gleaned from onthisday.com, including the inventions of margarine and corrugated cardboard, the founding of the first ever Masonic lodge for Black American men, and the lynching of eighteen Chinese immigrants by a mob of approximately five hundred people in L.A.

'Turn It On': The italicised phrases are taken from the lyrics to the 1997 song 'Turn It On', by Sleater-Kinney.

'Pacific Pocket Mouse': This species of mouse, the smallest in North America, is classified as endangered; according to Wikipedia, only about 150 individuals currently exist.

'Scenes From *Sherlock Holmes and the Pearl of Death*': The title *Sherlock Holmes and the Pearl of Death* is taken from the 1944 film of the same name, directed by Roy William Neill.

'Public House': This poem takes its title from the film *Public House* (2016), a documentary by Sarah Turner about the Ivy House pub in Peckham, London, and was commissioned for use in the film.

'Installation': This poem was prompted by works in various media by David Escalona, as shown at Copperfield Gallery, London, in 2016 and elsewhere.

'Eight Scenes From an Exhibition': Some of the works described in this poem are loosely derived from pieces by Félix González-Torres, Hilma af Klint, Rachel Maclean, and Kara Walker; others are wholly imaginary.

'Rabbit Empire': This poem was inspired by David Lynch's 2006 film *Inland Empire*.